Young Helen Keller

Woman of Courage

A Troll First-Start® Biography

by Anne Benjamin
illustrated by Julie Durrell

Troll Associates

Library of Congress Cataloging-in-Publication Data

Benjamin, Anne.
     Young Helen Keller: woman of courage / by Anne Benjamin;
illustrated by Julie Durrell.
          p.   cm.—(First-start biographies)
     Summary: A simple biography of the blind and deaf woman who spent
her life writing and helping others with similar disabilities.
     ISBN 0-8167-2530-6 (lib. bdg.)   ISBN 0-8167-2531-4 (pbk.)
     1. Keller, Helen, 1880-1968—Juvenile literature.   2. Blind-deaf—
United States—Biography—Juvenile literature.   [1. Keller, Helen,
1880-1968.   2. Blind.   3. Deaf.   4. Physically handicapped.]
I. Durrell, Julie, ill.   II. Title.   III. Series.
HV1624.K4B43   1992
362.4'1'092—dc20
[B]   91-26406

Helen Keller could not hear or see.
Yet she helped many people in her
amazing life.

Helen was born in Tuscumbia,
Alabama on June 27, 1880.
She was a happy, healthy baby.

But when she was almost 2 years old,
Helen became very sick.

In time, Helen got well. But her
illness left her deaf and blind.
Helen felt all alone in a dark
and silent world.

Because Helen could not hear,
she also could not talk. She had
no way to tell other people how
she felt or what she thought.

Helen did not know other people had feelings. She often hit or kicked other children.

Once, Helen even pushed her baby
sister Mildred out of her cradle.

Helen's parents knew Helen needed
help. They took her to see Dr.
Alexander Graham Bell. Today,
Dr. Bell is remembered for inventing
the telephone. But when Helen's
parents came to him, he was running
a school to help people teach the deaf.

11

Dr. Bell said there was a special way deaf people could "talk" by making signs with their fingers. He told the Kellers how to find a teacher to help Helen.

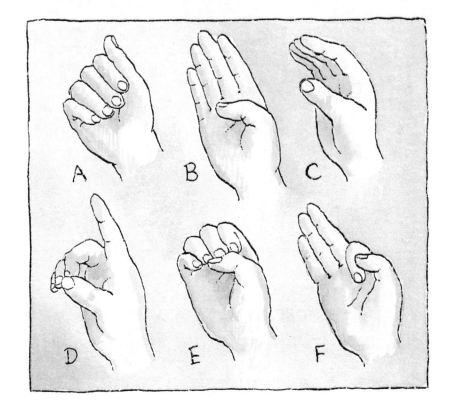

When Helen was 7, a woman named
Annie Sullivan came to live with the
Kellers. She would change Helen's life.

Annie knew what it was like not
to be able to see. She had been
nearly blind when she was a child.
She had had 2 operations to save
some of her eyesight.

Annie began teaching Helen
right away. She gave Helen
a doll. Then she spelled d-o-l-l
in Helen's hand.

17

Every day, Annie spelled words into
Helen's hand. Helen learned quickly.
But she did not know she was making
words. She still could not "talk" to
people.

Annie and Helen had many fights.
Annie wanted Helen to obey her,
and Helen did not like this!

Helen was used to doing what she wanted. Her parents felt sorry for her. They never punished her when she was bad.

At mealtime, Helen ate with her
fingers and grabbed other people's
food. Annie made her use a fork
and spoon and eat her own food.

Annie treated Helen just like any other child. And every day Helen behaved a little better.

24

One day, Annie took Helen out to the water pump. While water poured over one of Helen's hands, Annie spelled w-a-t-e-r into the other. Suddenly, Helen understood what words were. Her life would never be the same.

Now Helen could "talk" to people.
And they could "talk" to her.

Helen wanted to know everything she
could about the world. Annie could not
answer Helen's questions fast enough.

27

Helen learned to read and write in
Braille. In Braille, words are printed
in raised dots that blind people can
feel, or "read," with their fingers.

She also learned to lip-read by
touching people's faces. And when
she was a teenager, Helen even
learned to speak.

When Helen was 20, she did
something that many people thought
was impossible. She went to college.
Annie went with her to help her study.

Helen spent her life helping blind
and deaf people. She gave speeches
and wrote many books.

Helen Keller died on June 1, 1968.
But people all over the world still
remember her courageous, helpful life.